KT-451-075

060770

THE HENLEY COLLEGE LIBRARY

Raintree is an imprint of Capstone Global Library Limited, a company incorporated in England and Wales having its registered office at 7 Pilgrim Street, London, EC4V 6LB – Registered company number: 6695582

To contact Raintree, please phone 0845 6044371, fax + 44 (0) 1865 312263, or email myorders@raintreepublishers.co.uk.

Text © Capstone Global Library Limited 2013
First published in hardback in 2013
The moral rights of the proprietor have been asserted.

All rights reserved. No part of this publication may be reproduced in any form or by any means (including photocopying or storing it in any medium by electronic means and whether or not transiently or incidentally to some other use of this publication) without the written permission of the copyright owner, except in accordance with the provisions of the Copyright, Designs, and Patents Act 1988 or under the terms of a licence issued by the Copyright Licensing Agency, Saffron House, 6–10 Kirby Street, London EC1N 8TS (www.cla. co.uk). Applications for the copyright owner's written permission should be addressed to the publisher.

Edited by Andrew Farrow, Adrian Vigliano, and Vaarunika Dharmapala
Designed by Philippa Jenkins
Original illustrations © Capstone Global Library Limited 2013
Illustrated by HL Studios and Alvaro Fernandez Villa Advocate-Art pp4-5
Picture research by Mica Brancic
Printed and bound in China

ISBN 978 1 406 26092 2
17 16 15 14 13
10 9 8 7 6 5 4 3 2 1

British Library Cataloguing in Publication Data
Gogerly, Liz.
A world after fossil fuels.
333.7'94-dc23
A full catalogue record for this book is available from the British Library.

Acknowledgements
We would like to thank the following for permission to reproduce photographs: Alamy pp 11 (© Art Directors & TRIP), 12 (© Everyday Images), 16 (© JFP), 19 (© epa european pressphoto agency b.v.), 26 (© AF archive), 31 (© PhotoStock-Israel/Asaf Sultan), 41 (© Thomas Jackson); Corbis pp 14 (VII/© Ashley Gilbertson), 15 (Demotix/© Tom Craig), 18 (epa/© Juan Carlos Hidalgo), 24 (© Ashley Cooper), 29 (© Frans Lanting), 33 (Demotix/© Majdi Fathi), 34 (epa/© Piyal Adhikary), 40 (imagebroker/© Daniel Schoenen), 44 (Dagens Naringsliv/© Orjan F. Ellingvag), 46 (Blend Images/© KidStock); Getty Images pp 7 (Time & Life Pictures/Allan Tannenbaum), 20 (AFP/ Marc Hofer), 21 (AFP/Adek Berry), 23 (Matthew Peyton), 39 (Robert Nickelsberg); Press Association p 43 (AP Photo/Josh Reynolds); Reuters p 25 (Dave Amit); Science Photo Library p 47 (Detlev Van Ravenswaay).

Design features throughout courtesy of Shutterstock: empty cork memo board, background (© Reinhold Leitner), storm clouds (© KavardakovA), chain link fence (© ARENA Creative).

Cover photograph of a pile of used cars reproduced with permission of Shutterstock (© Fortish).

We would like to thank Michael Mastrandrea for his invaluable help in the preparation of this book.

Every effort has been made to contact copyright holders of material reproduced in this book. Any omissions will be rectified in subsequent printings if notice is given to the publisher.

Disclaimer
All the internet addresses (URLs) given in this book were valid at the time of going to press. However, due to the dynamic nature of the internet, some addresses may have changed, or sites may have changed or ceased to exist since publication. While the author and publisher regret any inconvenience this may cause readers, no responsibility for any such changes can be accepted by either the author or the publisher.

THE WORLD WAKES UP

If there were a serious and long-term disruption to oil supplies in the Middle East, how would it affect us? What would the world be like without enough fossil fuels? The story you are about to read is just one idea of how things might develop in this situation. No one can know for sure how the world will cope as we run out of fossil fuels, and things could turn out very differently.

After reports of trouble in the Middle East in 2020, the first reaction is concern about petrol. News alerts on television, radio, and the internet about the terrorist attacks in the Gulf make everyone think about the effect on fuel supplies. The headlines provoke anxiety. Although there is no immediate fuel shortage, queues begin to form at petrol stations around the world as people rush out to fill up their tanks. In 2020, people have a different mindset from us today. They are more aware that world oil supplies are running out. The terrorist attacks in the Middle East force them to pay attention to a crisis that had been looming for a long time.

Pouring oil on troubled waters

Behind the scenes, world leaders work towards a solution. They conduct emergency meetings to make back-up plans. Talks with the leaders of **OPEC (Organization of the Petroleum Exporting Countries)** are top of the agenda. Chief executives of multinational fuel companies are hauled into meetings to discuss oil reserves and how to manage the crisis. There is panic in high places, but politicians tell the public to keep calm. However, it's only a matter of time before people question the leaders' power to pour oil on troubled water…

WHAT WOULD YOU DO?

Buying fuel

In an oil crisis, would you rush out to buy fuel? Would you listen to the news and join the panic, or would you remain calm and think that your government would have the situation under control?

HOW LIKELY IS IT?

A sudden world oil crisis

In 1973, Americans were confronted with a serious oil crisis. It began with the 1973 Arab-Israeli War, also known as the Yom Kippur War.

Fighting between Israel and a coalition of Egypt and Syria began in October 1973. The Arab members of OPEC declared an oil embargo (banned the trade of oil) on the United States when it re-supplied the Israeli military. Between October 1973 and March 1974, Arab oil producers ceased to supply oil to the United States. The embargo was later extended to other Western countries and to Japan. The Arab nations wanted to put pressure on the United States to withhold support from the Israelis.

Emergency measures

The US government, under President Richard Nixon, did not give in to the Arab nations' demands and the United States was plunged into an oil crisis.

Huge queues at petrol stations became normal. Within a month, the price of petrol quadrupled. People rallied and attempted to cut their consumption of oil. Nixon requested that petrol stations stopped selling petrol on Saturday nights and Sundays. Together with emergency measures such as lowering the speed limit to 88 kilometres (55 miles) per hour, Americans managed to lower oil consumption by about 20 per cent. Rationing was under consideration but the crisis ended before it could be implemented.

Once the embargo was lifted, the price of fuel fell and people returned to their everyday lives. However, long-term effects of the crisis in the United States include the production of more fuel-efficient cars and oil heating being gradually replaced by electric heating.

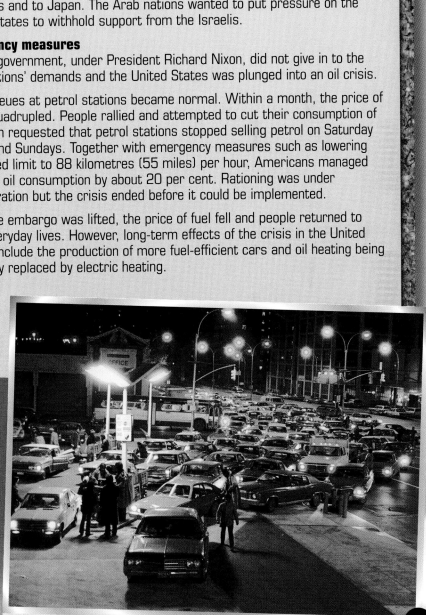

↗

These cars are queueing for petrol in January 1974 during the oil crisis.

An oil crisis of the future

The 1973 oil crisis lasted about six months. The oil crisis in 2020 is about to set the world in turmoil. In 2020, the challenge is dealing with an oil crisis at a time when there is less oil overall.

For many years, experts, especially **geologists**, have warned us about the time when oil production will go into decline. This means that the amount of oil that is extracted each day will go down and the cost of oil will go up. They predict that the decline in oil will occur after we have reached "peak oil". Peak oil is the time when oil production is at its highest. Some experts believe that once we have reached peak oil, we have about 20 years before supplies run out. However, nobody knows for sure. In the year 2020, discussions about an impending oil crisis are regularly in the news. People quickly realize that this situation is going to be grave.

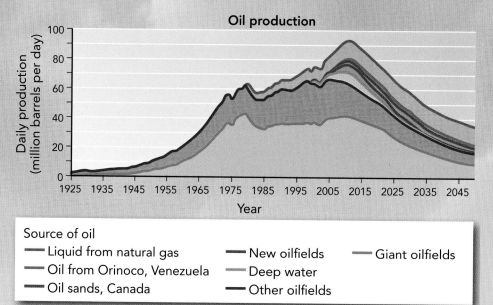

Oil production

Daily production (million barrels per day) vs Year

Source of oil
- Liquid from natural gas
- Oil from Orinoco, Venezuela
- Oil sands, Canada
- New oilfields
- Deep water
- Other oilfields
- Giant oilfields

The domino effect

In the future, it may be a wave of terrorist bombs or a natural disaster that triggers an energy crisis. Panic at the petrol pumps would be the first symptom of the crisis. Rising transport costs would affect food distribution. Inevitably, shops and businesses would close. So much of modern society is based on burning oil that it isn't difficult to see how an oil crisis could escalate into a full-scale crisis.

This graph shows estimated world oil production from 1925–2045. According to this projection, we reached peak oil in about 2010 and oil production is now in decline.

Scientists can't accurately predict when peak oil will happen. Matthew Simmons, author of a 2005 book called *Twilight in the Desert: The Coming Saudi Oil Shock and the World Economy*, reckons: "peaking is one of these fuzzy events that you only know clearly when you see it through a rear view mirror, and by then an alternate resolution is generally too late."

Some experts think that we reached the peak of easy-to-drill **crude oil** in 2004. Others have estimated it could be any time between 2006 and 2016. Reaching peak oil does not mean the end of oil supplies, but it heralds an age when there will not be enough oil to meet demand, a situation that will cause further fuel inflation.

World crude oil consumption by year

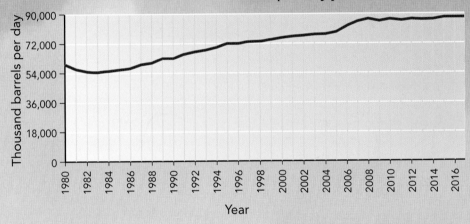

Crisis management

How well we would really cope with such a situation in the future depends upon what happens in the world between now and when (and if) a crisis occurs. On the positive side, scientists have been coming up with alternatives to petroleum-based fuels for decades. In 2011, annual oil demand in the United States actually fell. However, global demand for oil continued to rise, especially in newly industrialized nations such as China and India.

This diagram shows that oil consumption has steadily increased from the mid-1980s to 2012. The world could survive a fuel crisis in the future if demand for oil fell in line with the supply of oil.

Balance of power

As we have seen, meetings between world leaders and major oil companies are focused on handling the situation. Another important matter they look at is oil reserves. Oil reserves are the estimated quantity of crude oil that can be extracted in a commercially viable way. Saudi Arabia has the largest proven oil reserves in the world, followed by Venezuela, Canada, Iran, Iraq, and Kuwait. As most of the oil reserves in the world are in the Middle East, a terrorist situation in that area has a dramatic effect on Western industrial nations. Industry is dependent on crude oil. Even a short-term disruption to oil supplies has the power to damage the world's major economies.

PRODUCTS MADE FROM OIL

- petrol
- plastics
- solvents
- cosmetics
- drugs
- paint
- detergents
- ink
- pesticides
- fabric

Ordinary people want answers about what is going to happen next. Many question the importance of oil and whether other fossil fuels can be utilized in the crisis. In the year 2020, people are more aware of the **scarcity** of fossil fuels. They understand there is a connection between fossil fuels and climate change. They are anxious about environmental issues, but since the **Industrial Revolution** fossil fuels have played a major part in our lives, such that we have become dependent on them.

Fossil fuels facts

The world's fossil fuels include coal, oil, and natural gas. These are made from the fossilized remains of prehistoric plants and animals. They were formed millions of years ago and usually need to be extracted from under ground. They are called **non-renewable resources** because they are produced naturally only at a very slow rate so cannot be replaced. Coal has been used for heat and cooking for thousands of years, and deposits can be found all around the world. Known as black gold, it powered the Industrial Revolution.

However, as important as coal has been in the industrialization of the world, it is not a good oil replacement. Coal can be turned into a petrol-like fuel for vehicles but the process for making this fuel is energy intensive. Coal also emits up to twice the amount of **carbon dioxide** as oil, which means it contributes more to **global warming**. One day, coal will also run out. Some scientists think global peak coal may take place in about 200 years' time.

NATURAL GAS

Natural gas is another fossil fuel that has been used since ancient times. Natural gas vehicles (NGVs) can run on liquefied natural gas (LNG) or compressed natural gas (CNG). In 2010, there were about 12.67 million NGVs on the road and 18,200 filling stations worldwide. Natural gas contributes less to global warming, so in theory it is a good replacement for oil. However, there is the question of peak gas. In 2008, the US Energy Information Administration predicted growth until 2030, after which, natural gas production may go into decline.

This is an **oil refinery** in Saudi Arabia. Some experts predict that Saudi Arabia will reach peak oil in the near future.

Fuel theft

At the start of the oil crisis, the first people to feel the pinch are the less well-off. Despite fuel inflation, the wealthy can afford to fuel their vehicles. As the days go by, the economic divide adds to the tension. In the United Kingdom, in 2011, insurance companies and breakdown rescue services reported a small rise in fuel theft. Thieves cut through fuel lines, broke open fuel caps, removed petrol tanks, or used pumping equipment to steal petrol. In 2020, the rise in fuel theft is blamed on the rising cost of petrol.

Within weeks, petrol becomes so scarce and expensive that fuel theft is a more everyday occurrence. The streets are a danger zone where armed thieves look for easy targets. Cars parked on the road are like sitting ducks. Fuel tanks left unguarded can be easily plundered. Some thieves steal to satisfy their own needs. Organized groups steal in bulk to supply the **black market**. Anyone with a full tank of fuel needs to be security conscious and vigilant at all times.

How low will people go in a crisis? Siphoning petrol from another car is quick and easy and becomes more commonplace as desperation sets in.

Protest on the streets

Panic leads to protest. Many people vent their frustration at rising fuel costs by holding protest marches. Much of their anger is directed at the governments of the world. Around the globe, groups of protesters form outside council and government buildings. In the past, these kinds of protests were generally against rising fuel duty or to voice concerns about the environment. Now, people are pleading for more oil. There are scenes of chaos and confusion. Protesting doesn't bring them the answers or results they need. There is a rising feeling of unrest, instability, helplessness, and impending doom.

HOW LIKELY IS IT?

A fuel panic

In March 2012, the United Kingdom experienced a fuel panic that had the potential to bring the nation to a standstill. Since 2000, a series of fuel protests have taken place in the country in response to rising fuel costs. In 2005, protests resulted in some panic buying on the part of the public. However, panic buying in 2012 occurred as a result of the mere threat of a protest by petrol tanker drivers. Their dispute was over working conditions and employment contracts; there was no shortage of fuel, and a strike had not been organized.

The panic started when government minister Francis Maude told the public they should have full tanks of petrol and "maybe a little in their garage as well in a jerry can". Thousands of motorists rushed to petrol stations to fill up, even though it would be many days before a strike could begin.

Within days, petrol sales rose by 170 per cent. All over the country, stations ran dry. There were scenes of "fuel rage" as people got angry with each other at petrol stations. The army was put on standby in case there was a national emergency. The strike never went ahead, but this fuel crisis demonstrated how quickly people could be panicked into buying fuel they didn't immediately need.

PANIC SETS IN

By the second week of the crisis, the reality has hit home for millions. There is less traffic on the roads. Many people have stopped using their cars because they can't afford to fill them up with petrol or **diesel**. By 2020, there are more vehicles using **biofuel** and electric cars. There are also some magnetically controlled cars and cars run on compressed air. However, these are expensive alternatives and the majority have not made the switch to this new technology. In the past, biofuel was lauded as the replacement for petrol and diesel. In the current situation, it's clear that the world has not done enough to make the transition to biofuels.

Many people have started to accept that life is not going to return to normal. Millions of people who usually use their cars to get to work are stranded at home. Meanwhile, some people have become more resourceful. A group of New York commuters have set up a website to promote car sharing. The idea is catching on everywhere. More people are getting on their bikes again. Sales of bicycles have rocketed; in some places, the only way you'll get a new bike is on the black market.

The 2003 oil crisis in Iraq meant fuel prices increased and rationing had to be introduced. Queues of over a mile were reported at some petrol stations.

Can we make biofuels from seaweed?

Biofuels are produced from **renewable resources** such as plant **biomass**, vegetable oils, and waste materials. Bioethanol is made from crops such as corn or sugarcane and is currently the most commonly available biofuel worldwide. Biodiesel is produced from vegetable oils and animal fats and it is the most common biofuel in Europe. In 2011, scientists at the Bio Architecture Lab in California, USA made a breakthrough in microbe research which allowed them to convert seaweed to ethanol. Biofuel from seaweed could help to solve a future oil crisis. Seaweed is fast growing and plentiful in coastal areas. At the moment, the processing of seaweed to ethanol is expensive. Ben Graziano of the Carbon Trust believes that seaweed could be a great alternative to other biofuels: "The potential is certainly there, not least because most of the Earth is covered in water. If they can get the scale up and the costs down, it has huge potential."

By 2020, there may be more cars like this Renault electric micro car – but will they survive an oil crisis any better than petrol cars?

Electric cars at a standstill

All around the world, there is an increase in car hijacks. Expensive electric cars are the most vulnerable. Electric car owners have become more cautious and are scared to go out in their vehicles. As the fuel crisis continues, it's apparent just how reliant these so-called environmentally friendly cars are on fossil fuels, too. Until recently, replacement engine parts for electric cars were delivered by lorries run on diesel. Now that the price of diesel has quadrupled, the lorries aren't making the deliveries. It's only a matter of time before the electric car is grounded, too.

Shops run dry

Fewer lorries means the delivery of all supplies is breaking down. Panic buying of all commodities is adding to the crisis. Staples such as bread, dairy products, fresh fruit and vegetables, and toiletries are flying off the supermarket shelves. Shipments of food from around the world are severely affected and imported goods are incredibly expensive. Some governments are imposing emergency measures such as rationing to ensure a fair distribution of food, clothes, and other goods. Looting and theft is on the increase. The UK and US governments have been forced to introduce **curfews** to maintain public order. In Italy, the army has fired water cannons to break up a huge crowd of desperate, angry people who had queued unsuccessfully to buy bread.

Reality bites: empty supermarket shelves mean many people struggle to feed themselves during the crisis.

WHAT WOULD YOU DO?

Stocking up with food

What would you do if your local supermarkets didn't have any more fresh fruit and vegetables? Perhaps you'd seek out locally grown food? How long would it be before you decided you would have to start growing your own provisions?

LOO ROLL RUNS OUT

In 1973, during the oil crisis in the United States, people began buying toilet rolls after a comedian on television joked that there would be a shortage. On this occasion, it was people's panic buying that actually caused the shortage. Normal delivery of toilet rolls resumed after a few weeks.

FACT OR FICTION?

Ghost town

"Lyndhurst was a ghost town, almost. There were no money-bringing tourists now, and the Forest [the New Forest], wilder than before, did not provide enough income to support a community. They boomed down deserted streets, left and left again. An old man leaning on a staff watching sheep graze a stretch of close-nibbled common turned at the sound of the motor, shook his fist at them and shouted something indistinguishable. But a curse, for certain."

Taken from *The Changes: The Weathermonger* by Peter Dickinson (Victor Gollancz, 1968). The novel is about an England that has been forced back to a medieval way of life, where machines are seen as the enemy.

Small businesses shut down

Towns and cities throughout the world are quieter and scarier places. There is an ever-present danger of being mugged or having a bag of precious food being snatched by thieves. There is less traffic and many more pedestrians and people using their bicycles. However, everyone seems to be in a rush to get home to safety. The old and sick have retreated inside and rely upon others to help them. Small businesses such as cafes, bars, and shops are closing down. Boarded up premises add to the general air of doom and gloom. In the United States and Australia, many remote towns and regions have become cut off from the rest of the country. Some places are being abandoned altogether to become no-go, ghost towns.

THE HENLEY COLLEGE LIBRAR

Chaos in the skies

The oil crisis has an immediate effect on the airline industry. In 2010, the shutting down of airspace over northern Europe (see panel below) caused widespread chaos. This crisis lasted for six days, but in a world suffering from an oil crisis the situation is more serious. Flights all around the world are cancelled. In 2020, some airlines have alternative renewable jet fuels (see panel opposite), but most have not made a full transition. At first, there are chaotic scenes at airports as stranded travellers try to make their way home. Within days, non-emergency flights are subject to cancellation or delay. Within weeks, trade, tourism, and other businesses are severely affected.

HOW LIKELY IS IT?

Would a crisis in air travel affect the world economy?

In April 2010, Iceland's Eyjafjallajökull's volcano erupted, creating an ash cloud that covered parts of northern Europe. Although the eruption was relatively small, it caused the largest shut-down of air traffic since World War II. The fine, sharp ash particles posed a safety risk to aircraft, so airspace was closed for six days across much of Europe. Over 100,000 flights were cancelled and, according to the International Air Transport Association (IATA), the airline industry lost an estimated US$1.7 billion.

Millions of passengers struggled to find alternative ways of getting home. International trade was also affected, especially the transportation of perishable goods such as vegetables and flowers. Many economies around the world suffered as a consequence. African exporters of green beans alone lost an estimated US$3.9 million because of the shutdown! Now, imagine the scene in 2020 when the disruption would last much longer than six days. The effect on the world economy would be enormous.

During the 2010 volcanic eruption, air passengers all over the world were left stranded at airports.

HOW LIKELY IS IT?

Jet fuel from waste

Biofuel produced from waste is another potential solution for our energy needs in the future. Organic waste, such as rotting food, goes into landfill and gives off a gas called methane or landfill gas. Methane is a greenhouse gas which contributes to global warming. Serious research into utilizing these gases began in the 1970s. Rather than sending rubbish off to landfill, the waste can be converted to gas or fuel in machines called **anaerobic digesters**.

In 2012, British Airways announced its plans to convert Londoners' rubbish into jet fuel. The first plant is expected to open in 2015. The aim is to turn half a million tonnes of household waste into 50,000 tonnes of jet fuel every year. This would provide only about 2 per cent of the airline's current fuel needs, but if it is successful the airline proposes to extend the project.

On 19 June 2012, history is made when a KLM Royal Dutch Airlines plane makes the first transatlantic flight on biofuel.

Mass transit meltdown

By 2020, many rail networks around the world are still using electric and diesel locomotives. Diesel locomotives are used for pulling freight and passenger trains. The rising cost of diesel followed by shortages of fuel mean that many of these services are cancelled. The crisis also affects the power supply. Power cuts mean electric locomotives are unreliable. Rail passengers are getting frustrated with the skeleton service available. The lucky few who manage to get on trains have to pay highly inflated fares.

At goods stations everywhere, undelivered cargo is piling high. The stench from perishable goods that have started to rot is revolting. At night, thieves steal from the containers. Fewer supplies are reaching the consumers in towns, cities, and villages. In the 19th century, the coming of the railway revolutionized travel. In 2020, the crippled railway system is a massive wake-up call to everyone. People living in remote towns and cities feel more cut off than ever, while people living in urban areas feel there is no way out.

> "Back in 1989 I became deeply depressed when I concluded that our greatest scientific achievements will soon be forgotten and our most cherished moments will crumble to dust. But more so, I knew that my children would feel the pressure, and will likely suffer. That really hurt…"

Richard Duncan, the Institute of Energy and Man
Taken from *The Party's Over: Oil, War and the Fate of Industrial Societies* by Richard Heinberg (Claireview Books, 2005)

During the oil crisis, civil disturbances may force the army out onto the streets to keep the peace.

Communication disruption

Lack of transport for deliveries and unreliable power sources mean that all lines of communication are frequently disrupted. People want to know what their government is doing to solve the crisis. In turn, governments are using any channels possible to announce emergency measures such as curfews, rationing, car sharing, or issuing of permits to travel.

The army moves in

In the first few weeks of the crisis, there is a greater police presence in most places. However, the police have transport issues of their own. It's obvious they can't deal with rising fuel theft, car hijacks, looting, and other social disturbances alone. Serious unrest requires military intervention. Riots in the French cities of Paris and Amiens mean the army has taken over disused buildings for security purposes. Other nations have the army on stand-by in case of an emergency.

> "My father rode a camel. I drive a car. My son flies in a jet airplane. His son will ride a camel."
>
> **A Saudi saying**
> Taken from *The Party's Over: Oil, War and the Fate of Industrial Societies* by Richard Heinberg (Claireview Books, 2005)

In March 2012, Indonesian police clashed with protestors against the rise in fuel prices. Violent scenes like this could become common in the crisis.

POWER CUTS

A month after the terrorist attack, interruptions to the power supply are reported from all over the world. Countries such as Poland and Taiwan are still able to generate a large proportion of electricity from coal-fired power stations, because they have coal supplies.

People are asking why there's a problem when there's still so much coal in the ground. The problem is transporting the coal to power plants. And some countries are no longer exporting their coal, but keeping it for their own use.

HOW IS ELECTRICITY GENERATED?

Electricity is generated in power stations. Fossil-fuel power stations burn coal, natural gas, or oil to produce electricity. Nuclear power is another non-renewable source of energy. However, unlike fossil fuels, it's not likely to run out in the near future. Renewable power stations can be run on **hydropower**, solar heat, **geothermal heat**, and biomass.

In 2006, fossil fuels were still the most common fuels for electricity generation (see pie chart) worldwide.

Since the 1970s, scientists have warned that carbon dioxide from burning fossil fuels is causing global warming and climate change. Many governments have taken heed and are proposing to build more nuclear power stations as well as encouraging investment in alternative energy sources.

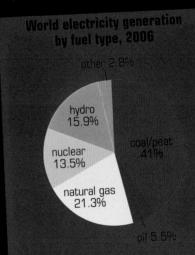

World electricity generation by fuel type, 2006

- other 2.8%
- hydro 15.9%
- coal/peat 41%
- nuclear 13.5%
- natural gas 21.3%
- oil 5.5%

WHAT WOULD YOU DO?

Home or export?

Norway has an abundance of renewable energy resources. As well as hydropower, the country has invested in solar, wind, and biomass power. In wetter years, Norway has enough "clean" energy to export to neighbouring countries such as Denmark. During an energy crisis, Norway may choose to use more of that capacity for its own needs. In this situation, would you supply your own people or honour the contracts to your overseas customers?

The energy winners

By 2020, many countries have already made a transition to renewable sources. These countries are set to handle the energy crisis better. Norway can generate over 99 per cent of its own electricity needs from hydropower, though it usually sells some of this electricity to other countries. Iceland derives about three-quarters of its electricity from geothermal power.

In many areas, demand for electricity is outstripping supply. In some places, blackouts are a daily occurrence. This is having a serious impact on business and manufacturing. Some regions have implemented changes such as planned brownouts (a temporary drop in voltage to avoid a blackout, which can cause lights to dim and damage some electrical equipment) or rolling blackouts (a series of planned blackouts at different times over a geographical region). People are getting used to using less electricity. They keep torches and candles ready for when the electricity goes off. It's no surprise that there's been an increase in the number of domestic fires and accidents!

GRID COLLAPSE

Electricity is generated at power stations and then distributed to users by the electricity distribution system, otherwise known as the grid. The grid is interconnected and allows us to share power. So, if one power station is not working to capacity or has to temporarily shut down, electricity can be taken from another part of the grid. However, the grid would struggle to cope if many power stations were not operating to capacity or their output was not shared via a **national grid**. When the grid can't cope, there's a blackout!

The New York blackout in 2003 lasted over 24 hours and caused chaos to transport, mobile phone networks, water supply, and industry.

Global picture

Nations that began managing the transition from fossil fuels to a low-energy, **sustainable** society earlier in the century are coping reasonably well in the crisis. Some rural communities in less-developed countries are also doing better because they have always had a way of living that doesn't rely upon huge energy consumption. Industrial nations that refused to move with the times are the worst affected.

Solar energy

Advances in solar power technology mean that many countries and communities have already built solar power stations or added **photovoltaic** installations to buildings and homes. Since the 1970s, solar power has worked well for small communities or people living in remote regions that are not connected to the power grid.

Small communities in sunny places such as Africa are adjusting to the crisis well. They suffer shortfalls of electricity on cloudy days, but are learning to cut back when required. Residents of California, USA, have long embraced solar power and can boast more solar panels on homes than any other US state. Development of solar power stations increased in the first decades of the 2000s. By 2020, industrial nations such as Germany, the United States, and Spain are well advanced in providing solar power. Developing nations such as China and India are also utilizing energy from the Sun.

This solar panel has been placed on the roof of a simple village home in the Anti-Atlas mountains of Morocco, North Africa.

WHAT IS SOLAR POWER?

The Sun is Earth's major source of energy. Light and heat from the Sun sustains nearly all forms of life on the planet. Solar power is electricity generated via solar panels from sunlight. A solar panel contains groups of button-sized devices called solar cells. Light from the Sun causes electrons to jump between the cells to create a flow of electricity. Solar thermal power uses the Sun's energy to heat a liquid which is then used to generate steam and turn a turbine, generating electricity. The problem with solar power is how to store it so that it can be used at night-time or when the Sun isn't shining. Scientists continue to investigate effective ways of storing the Sun's heat.

The Gujarat Solar Farm is a group of solar parks in northern India. In 2012, the park was proclaimed to be the biggest solar park in Asia. At this time, the park covered about 2,000 hectares (about 4,900 acres), with a generation capacity amounting to two-thirds of India's solar power production. In 2012, the Indian government announced plans to extend the park further into the desert.

Nuclear power

Nuclear power is sustaining the national grid in some places. Most stations are able to remain operational. Nuclear fuels are transported by rail in huge transport flasks. Despite the upheaval of the railway networks, governments everywhere have prioritized the transportation of nuclear fuels and the other goods needed to run the plants.

One major problem is how to dispose of **radioactive** waste safely. This is a costly procedure that consumes large amounts of energy, but many governments have apportioned the funds required. Nuclear power can't pick up the slack when fossil-fuelled power stations close down, but some governments are looking at their long-term nuclear programmes again. They have halted decommissioning (the closure) of remaining plants and plan to develop more nuclear power stations in the future.

↗

In *Mad Max 2: The Road Warrior* (1981), the world is plunged into chaos when oil begins to run out. In the future, can we expect the same to happen in real life?

In 2011, France was able to generate about 77 per cent of its electricity from nuclear power. By 2020, this figure is even higher. The government has managed the situation by forcing cuts on domestic and industrial use. They have also apportioned reserves of petrol and diesel for the safe disposal of radioactive waste. It has been a sacrifice people have been happy to make.

1986 CHERNOBYL DISASTER

Nuclear power took off in the 1960s and 1970s. At this time, nuclear energy was lauded as a cheap, pollution-free alternative to fossil fuels. Accidents such as the 1886 **Chernobyl disaster** in the Soviet Union made many more people question the safety of nuclear power. In 2011, after the accident at the Fukushima nuclear plant in Japan, Germany and Switzerland announced plans to phase out nuclear power stations. Nations such as Australia, Denmark, and Italy already opposed plans to develop nuclear power.

Wind power

Nations that invested in wind power in the past are reaping the rewards now. The United Kingdom, the United States, China, Spain, Denmark, and Germany scaled up operations in the early 2000s. Turbines and wind farms already connected up to the grid are generating upwards of one-quarter of the electricity supplied in some regions. Wind is a vital resource during the crisis. In the past, many people complained about wind farms, claiming they ruined the appearance of the countryside. They blamed wind turbines at sea for killing wildlife. During the crisis, many people are not so quick to criticize this valuable resource and there is a rush to complete existing building projects.

WHAT IS WIND POWER?

Humans have been using wind energy for thousands of years. Before the industrial age, windmills were the only way to grind grain other than by hand. The modern version of the windmill is the wind turbine. It needs wind to turn its blades to generate electricity. A wind farm is a group of wind turbines in the same place. Most wind farms are situated in open countryside or **offshore**, where there are no obstacles to wind flow.

Wind power is free, but the cost of building turbines and other infrastructure is high. Technical problems arise because the wind changes from day to day. This means wind power cannot be guaranteed to take up the slack during a peak in energy demand. However, wind power has great potential and scientists continue to research ways of harnessing and storing wind power.

Hydroelectricity

Hydroelectricity is another guarantee during the crisis. Some of the largest hydroelectric facilities in the world are in China, Brazil, Venezuela, and the United States. An oil crisis is no impediment to the flow of water and these massive hydroelectric plants continue to operate to capacity. China invested in at least 15 major dam projects between 2012 and 2020, and many of these facilities are up and running and supplying electricity to China's insatiable industrial economy. A poor, less developed South American nation, Paraguay, is an unexpected winner. It produces all of its electricity from hydroelectric dams and exports its excess to Brazil and Argentina.

"WHITE COAL"

Hydropower is often called white coal because of its abundance and potential power. In the 20th century, hydroelectric dams were built across many major rivers throughout the world. In 2012, water was still the most commonly used renewable resource for generating electricity. However, the potential for building more large dams is hampered by production costs and also the negative impact on the environment.

In the future, there will be more run-of-the-river hydroelectric power stations. These plants are positioned next to rivers but do not require a large reservoir of stored water. Tidal power is another growth area, where the energy created by the tides of the sea is converted to power. Micro hydro plants using smaller rivers and streams will also become more common as they are more practical and can be installed quickly.

Electric solutions

It is a few months after the crisis began and the world is still coming to terms with the disruption to the market in fossil fuels. International leaders, industrialists, and engineers gather daily to discuss how to get the most out of the resources they have.

They are also talking about long-term solutions for their countries. Experts are called in to give guidance and advice about energy resources. Politicians and businesses are now taking much more seriously the advice about radical changes to energy policy. In the past, they ignored inconvenient truths that would be unpopular with taxpayers and voters or cost their businesses. The options for each nation are very different. However, one thing is clear: most countries need to invest more money if they want the world to restore stability. And, at this time, money is tight. Many industries and businesses have gone bust and some financial markets look set to crash.

The Itaipú Dam on the Parana River between Brazil and Paraguay was opened in 1984. It is the largest development of its kind in the world.

FACT OR FICTION?

Persuading leaders to make changes

"For an unnaturally large fee, he was to address an energy conference attended by institutional investors, pension-fund managers, solid types who would not be easily persuaded that the world, their world, was in danger and that they should align their investment patterns accordingly. Through inertia, blind professional custom, they were bound to their old familiars, oil, gas, coal, forestry. He was to persuade them that what they currently made profitable would one day destroy them."

From *Solar* by Ian McEwan, published by Jonathan Cape. Reprinted by permission of the Random House Group Limited.

ONE YEAR ON

One year on, and the world remains a tense and unstable place. Many nations have economies that are suffering from the disruption to industry and trade. The tension between many nations rests on the issue of fuel supply. Some nations' energy supplies balance on a knife-edge, depending upon diplomatic relations with oil-rich nations in the Middle East or gas-rich nations such as Russia. Once upon a time, the most powerful nations in the world were the industrialized nations; now it is the countries that control energy supplies.

HOW LIKELY IS IT?
Would Russia withhold its energy supplies?

Russia holds the largest reserves of natural gas and is the leading producer and exporter of natural gas in the world. In 2006, Russia's dominant, state-run gas supplier Gazprom switched off its supply to neighbouring Ukraine. Tensions had been high between Russia and the Ukraine for years. Ukrainians disputed paying more for natural gas than other European countries. Meanwhile, about 80 per cent of natural gas destined for these European nations transited through pipelines across the Ukraine. The situation became worse when the Russians accused the Ukrainians of diverting gas intended for other countries and using it for their own needs.

This crisis was swiftly resolved, but another major dispute erupted in 2008. On 1 January 2009, the dispute intensified and Russia cut off all supplies to Europe via the Ukrainian pipeline. Many eastern European domestic users were badly affected because the shut down came in the middle of a freezing cold winter. Gas prices fluctuated throughout Europe. By 21 January, gas supplies were resumed but the crisis was a wake-up call to other European nations dependent upon Russian gas. In the event of a world energy crisis, Russia would probably react in the same way as it did in 2009.

Food rationing means tight control of staples such as pulses, meat, and dairy products. Here, lentils are being measured out for customers.

Food crisis

Food has been running out. In the early days of the crisis, transporting goods was the problem, but there were stores of food that could be distributed, sometimes under government control. Now, the issue is food production. There isn't enough oil to fuel tractors and other farming machinery, and the shortage has also severely affected the manufacture of pesticides and fertilizers that rely on oil. Without these artificial means of increasing crop yields, there aren't enough crops for humans let alone animals. A knock-on effect is less meat and dairy products.

Starvation

Food manufacturing and processing has been disrupted, and many businesses dealing with non-essential supplies have gone bust. With air transport costs at a record high, some countries are critically hit because of a reliance on imported food. Demand for food has outstripped supply and the price of food has rocketed. Governments that haven't already introduced food rationing are now doing so.

Some people are trying to grow their own food. Soon, every available area of land is being planted, including gardens, parks, and football pitches! However, the majority of people living in industrial societies aren't geared up to grow enough food to supply their own needs. It takes years of readjustment and planning to resolve the problem. Not everyone has access to land – they rely on the good will and charity of others. Communities that band together are more successful. In the meantime, the quest to put food on our plates turns nasty. Food theft and scavenging is on the increase. Death from starvation, especially for the old and weak, is more common, too.

Water supply

Maintaining a supply of water has become a problem, too. Water treatment plants and pumping stations need energy. They also require maintenance and new components. Much of the water supply infrastructure is falling into disrepair and many places can no longer rely upon safe clean drinking water. Drinking untreated water can lead to deadly waterborne diseases such as cholera and dysentery.

Water conservation is another issue. Scientists have found that global warming is causing more frequent and severe droughts in some places around the world. Water management is key to keeping drought-stricken areas habitable. In the present crisis, desert cities such as Las Vegas and Los Angeles have become largely uninhabitable due to crippling shortages of water. People living next to lakes and rivers have a chance of survival but water treatment is still a problem.

FACT OR FICTION?

Starved for moisture

"We lived … in a time of drought and war. The great empires had fallen and been divided. The land was parched and starved for moisture, and the men who lived on it fought for every drop. Outside, the wind howled like something wounded. Inside, our skin flaked, and our eyes stung and burned. Our tongues were like thick snakes asleep in dark graves."

Excerpt taken from *The Water Wars* by Cameron Stracher (Sourcebooks Fire, 2011)

Health in crisis

The number of sick and dying has increased. Human life is more vulnerable than ever, but, at this time of great need, there is a decline in the standard of health care. Much modern medicine is dependent on oil. The main impact has been the transportation of drugs and other medical supplies. There are fewer emergency vehicles on the road. Many items, including synthetic rubber gloves and surgical instruments, are made using oil.

Meanwhile, hospitals need energy for heating, sterilization, and running medical equipment. Hospitals everywhere are prioritizing emergency and essential operations. Every country has its own health care system. In 2020, the countries that have already weaned themselves off oil dependency are in a fitter state.

HOW LIKELY IS IT?

Can hospitals cope with energy shortages?

In February 2012, the people of the Gaza Strip in the Middle East experienced the worst fuel shortage in years caused by an Israeli **blockade**. At first, it was drivers that were hit. Then there were electric blackouts and people in Gaza's hospitals suffered. Juan-Pedro Schaerer, the head of the International Committee of the Red Cross delegation for Israel and the territories, warned:

> "The current failure to ensure delivery of fuel and electricity could rapidly lead to interruptions in vital public services such as hospital care and water supply, putting the lives of thousands of patients in danger ... in the event of any such disruption, hospital operating theatres and specialist units, such as those providing intensive care, neonatal care and haemodialysis, would be especially hard hit."

In May 2012, there were reports of deaths and injuries caused by the fuel shortage. The crisis is, to date, ongoing.

↖ The energy crisis in the Gaza Strip meant there were blackouts lasting 18 hours a day in 2012. As a result, some premature infants received inadequate treatment in hospital.

The survivors

Who are the survivors of a society in turmoil? In some places, the black market for food and fuel helps to cater for those who can afford it. People living in the slums of developing countries or poor farmers in remote parts of Africa, Asia, and South America are coping better. These people have lived more sustainable lives than city dwellers for years. They have lots of small adaptable businesses that don't rely upon electricity. Carpenters use hand tools rather than power tools. Farmers till the land using animals rather than tractors.

Born into poverty, many of these people know how to survive on very little. They don't waste food and they recycle and reuse everything. These age-old skills have been passed down to them through the generations and are standing them in good stead during the energy crisis.

A boy in Calcutta, India makes a dollar a day by collecting empty plastic bottles and taking them to the recycling plant. Plastic bottles become more valuable in the crisis.

Fossil-free cities

In the 2000s, some countries and regions planned for a fossil-free future, and adapted their lives to be more eco-conscious. In 2020, many of these places are reaping the rewards of their forward planning. Such places already have power plants run on biomass or other renewable resources. They have solar installations on rooftops and roadsides to generate electricity and heat. Wind turbines are generating enough energy to power public buildings such as hospitals. High efficiency transit systems such as monorails run on electricity have replaced fuel-guzzling trains and buses. Some places have wider cycle paths and limits on car use in urban areas.

Meanwhile, some places have urban farms supplying citizens with locally produced food. In some towns, small businesses and shops have been purposely built to be a cycle-ride or walk away from these homes. Nowhere is immune to the energy crisis, but these cities and communities are more able to maintain a reasonable standard of living. These places are becoming the **template** for most of the world post-fossil fuels.

HOW LIKELY IS IT?

Fossil-free cities

Becoming a fossil-free city is no easy business but it is already happening in 2012. It takes years of planning and a change in thinking. The city of Växjö in Sweden converted its local power plant from oil to biomass in 1979. In 1996, the city pledged to become free of fossil fuels by 2030. Its three-pronged attack included energy conservation, development of renewable energy, and changing the habits of its citizens.

The city has the advantage of being surrounded by forests and lakes. Waste from the forest industry is burned at the local power plant to generate heat and power. Currently, 90 per cent of the energy used to heat the city and half of its electricity is derived from trees. In the past, the lakes around Växjö were badly polluted. These days, the sewage treatment plant pumps clean water into the lakes and converts sludge from the dirty water to biogas.

In the future, the city hopes to run its buses on locally produced biogas. In 2007, the BBC named Växjö "Europe's greenest city". Växjö's success relies upon careful urban planning, but it also requires people to take responsibility in their everyday lives. Initiatives include installing counters so people can monitor water, heat, and electricity consumption.

The world in 2020

This map shows some of the major events involved in our fictional energy crisis. Some countries remain relatively unaffected because they are rich in energy; others are suffering huge disruption to their way of life. Around the world, pollution levels have decreased as less fossil fuels are being burned. Without so many aeroplanes, the skies are quieter. Some experts are even claiming that the crisis might be a blessing in disguise for the future of the planet.

Canada: Canada has plenty of untapped oil within the oil sands in the province of Alberta.

Alaska

Alberta

Canada

NORTH AMERICA

USA

NORTH ATLANTIC OCEAN

PACIFIC OCEAN

Venezuela

SOUTH AMERICA

Paraguay

SOUTH ATLANTIC OCEAN

USA: Hydroelectric power, wind power, and solar power mean many parts of the USA have adapted well since the crisis began. However, areas such as southern California have plenty of solar energy but have become uninhabitable through drought and little access to water.

Venezuela: This South American country is not only rich in conventional oil but has massive oil sand deposits. In recent years Venezuela has become a leading economic power and the chief supplier of oil to the USA.

Paraguay: The Itaipú hydroelectric power plant generates more hydro electric power than any other hydroelectric power station in the world.

France: France's long-standing nuclear-energy programme means it still produces more nuclear power than any other nation. Slovakia, Switzerland, Belgium, and Hungary are also top producers.

Sweden: The fossil-free city of Växjö in Sweden has become the blueprint for sustainable cities all over the world.

China: The country remains a top industrial nation because it has made a successful transition to renewable energy while maintaining some of its large coal-fired power stations. The Three Gorges Dam on the Yangtze is the second largest hydroelectric power complex in the world.

UK: The UK leads the way with off-shore wind power energy.

ARCTIC OCEAN

Sweden

United Kingdom

EUROPE

France

ASIA

Spain

China

PACIFIC OCEAN

Saudi Arabia

United Arab Emirates

India

AFRICA

INDIAN OCEAN

AUSTRALASIA

SOUTHERN OCEAN

Spain: Spain leads the way with solar power in Europe. It exports a percentage of its output to Germany.

Saudi Arabia: Remains powerful because of its oil and gas reserves.

United Arab Emirates: The city of Masdar in the desert is an exemplary eco-city where wind and solar power meet human energy requirements. Even though the country is oil rich the cars in this city are powered by magnets.

India: India is a world leader in solar power and wind power. Solar power plants commissioned back in 2011/12 now supply nearly half of the nation's needs.

THE NEW WAY OF LIFE

It is five years after the crisis started, and some places have become uninhabitable. Millions of people have migrated in search of better lives. Journeys aren't easy. Many roads have fallen into disrepair. Meanwhile, journeys overseas are long and expensive, although still viable using wind power. Countries that had managed the transition to renewable resources and cities that had modelled themselves on successful fossil-free cities have become popular escapes. Some governments have responded to the new migration by shutting down borders or imposing stricter immigration laws.

Acceptance

Millions of people have accepted the changed circumstances and remained in their communities. They are learning to live with less energy and build their lives around the changes. These days, they are happy with enough food to survive, and there are a lot fewer obese people. People don't expect to be able to eat foods that cannot be produced locally.

In the same way, most people don't expect to fill their homes with electrical appliances and the latest must-have gadgets. Now that it's difficult and expensive to travel long distances, people are enjoying leisure time closer to home. This is bringing people and communities together. Some people even say that the change has been for the best!

Smaller communities have realized that the only way to survive is to make life more sustainable. In a world less mobile, it is vital for local communities to pull together. People have to share their skills and resources. Food production is crucial and many people have re-learned basic skills. At first, it was a challenge to make bread. Now the bread-making process starts with tilling the land and sowing the grain.

FACT OR FICTION?

A loaf of bread

" 'Look what I shot,' Gale holds up a loaf of bread with an arrow stuck in it, and I laugh. It's real bakery bread, not the flat, dense loaves we make from our grain rations. I take it in my hands, pull out the arrow, and hold the puncture in the crust to my nose, inhaling the fragrance that makes my mouth flood with saliva."

From THE HUNGER GAMES by Suzanne Collins, Scholastic Inc./Scholastic Press. Copyright © 2008 by Suzanne Collins. Reproduced by permission.

Experienced farmers have lent their knowledge. After harvesting, the grain is ground to make flour. The skills of trained engineers, carpenters, and builders have been called upon to build modern windmills. Finally, experienced bakers have had the job of making bread. By pulling together and working as a team, people have found the manpower, tools, and machinery they need for basic processing of food.

Organic farming methods would have to be used in a world without synthetic pesticides and fertilizers.

Farming and Foraging

Communities are farming with limited machinery and without synthetic pesticides and fertilizers. The fit and able work in the fields during sowing and harvest time. Many communities are growing fruit and vegetables. People are also adapting their diets. During World War II, people gathered wild rose hips to make syrup rich in vitamin C. In 2025, people are foraging for wild food such as mushrooms, herbs, and berries. People are also hunting for animals or go fishing. In places, this is threatening the survival of species, as some animals and birds are being hunted to extinction.

Housing

By 2025, most people have made their homes more sustainable. Communities and countries that developed energy-efficient passive buildings earlier in the century are doing better. Some places have whole housing schemes, schools, shops, and hospitals utilizing energy from the Sun. Meanwhile, many others can't afford the new technology. As in days of old, most governments are offering advice about **insulation**, and there are programmes to help people reduce energy consumption and install solar systems. In reality, millions of people are still living in cold or under-heated buildings.

 These passive solar houses in Germany may be how our homes of the future will look.

Around the home

New technology such as solar ovens and fridges run on biomass are replacing electric ovens and fridge freezers in some homes. Many cannot afford these new appliances, and production cannot easily meet demand. In some communities, people have to share cooking on open fires or old-fashioned style stoves that burn wood or coal. As a result, many areas of woodland are under threat. In some places, wood smoke is causing pollution and there are reports of smog.

WHAT WOULD YOU DO?

Daily living needs

Imagine yourself living in 2025 without the money to add solar panels to your home. What would you use to heat your home in the winter? What would you do to make food? Would you try to work together with other people in the community to meet your daily living requirements?

PASSIVE BUILDINGS

Passive homes and buildings are designed to have low energy needs. They have better insulation and an efficient ventilation system. They are designed to use the Sun's heat. For this reason, windows are positioned on the south-facing side of the building, while a sloped roof is built on the north side of the building to reduce heat loss. Meanwhile, solar panels on the roof and walls collect heat to be used in the house.

In 2012, there is estimated to be more than 37,000 passive houses worldwide, a tiny fraction of the housing stock. European countries such as Germany, Switzerland, Denmark, and Sweden are leaders in the field but passive housing is becoming popular in other countries. By 2025, some governments might make building to this standard compulsory.

Many people are using alternative food preservation techniques such as salting, pickling, or drying food. Waste management has become part of everyday life. Many more homes have **composters** under the sink and composter toilets; the compost is used on their own gardens or on community farms. People are throwing away less and reusing precious resources such as paper and glass. Anything that can't be reused is recycled.

Virtual lives

While, generally speaking, people are simplifying the way they live, others are more reliant on new technology than ever. Limited transport is pushing them towards virtual living. Electricity isn't a thing of the past, so computers and other technology can still be used. However, electricity is more expensive and less reliable. This is frustrating at a time when more people than ever are working from home using computers and video conferencing.

In the future, energy from the Sun will be used to charge mobile phones and other gadgets.

Industry and manufacturing

Many of the changes to everyday living have depended upon how industry has adapted during the crisis. At the beginning of the crisis, transport disruption led to the closure of many factories. People had less money and became more accustomed to reuse. The market forces of demand and supply drove many more manufacturers out of business, especially if they produced luxury goods. The petrochemical and petroplastic industries were reliant on oil, so now are much reduced in size and are under strict government control.

Economic growth

The demand for passive housing and new energy efficient technology has grown. Some new ventures have been able to organize the money, resources, and energy to supply these needs – often with the help of governments. In many countries, the manufacturing sector has revived. However, much of the new growth in the economy is from smaller local businesses, which are far more energy conscious than before. There are also more products made from renewable resources or recycled materials. One growth area is bioplastics.

Energy around us

Inventors and scientists are coming up with new ways of generating energy and making the best of limited resources. Some of the most bizarre ideas for generating energy actually work very well. Some gyms have hooked up to **generators**. All that running on treadmills, using exercise bikes, and energy burned off on rowing machines is being converted to electricity. Meanwhile, some crematoriums are converting the heat generated from burning corpses to electricity, or using it to heat buildings.

HOW LIKELY IS IT?

Bioplastics made from chicken feathers

Bioplastics can be made from plant-based oils such as soya bean, hemp, corn, and pea starch. Bioplastics are cheaper to make than petroplastics and are **biodegradable**. Currently, bioplastics are not as strong or durable as petroplastics but scientists are making advances all the time. One of the most exciting developments recently has been bioplastic from chicken feathers. Researchers at the University of Nebraska's Institute of Agriculture and Natural Resources have developed a plastic that is strong enough to be used for car bumpers and lasting enough to make mobile phone cases.

Post-2020, people will find more unusual ways of lighting up city streets. In 2010, a gas light in a park in Massachusetts is powered by the methane gas that is given off from dog poo!

The new spirit

Everyday life for many people is getting back on track. With societies and communities pulling together, there is a new spirit of survival. People are also finding ways of entertaining themselves in a world that has changed so much. They have been forced to seek out simpler pleasures. There is a renaissance of the arts and more appreciation of the natural world. In some places, there has been a total backlash against technology. Rather than tuning into iPods, people are rediscovering live music. There is more focus on personal fitness. People are valuing their possessions and cherishing each other more. Many people look back in horror at the **consumerism** and throwaway culture of the 20th century. Together, they are building a stronger, better, more sustainable future.

WHAT WOULD YOU DO?

Entertainment

Picture yourself in this new world in 2025. Imagine that you don't have the gadgets and electronic equipment that you take for granted now. What talents, skills, and hobbies would you fall back on? Do you think you would still enjoy yourself?

WHAT CAN WE DO?

In this book, we have presented some possible consequences of people struggling to cope with a shortage of oil and other fossil fuels. Some experts believe that we have already reached peak oil – which might suggest, although nobody knows for certain, that we have 20 years before we begin to run out. If this is the case, shouldn't everyone be doing more now to make our lives more sustainable?

Is there a problem?

Some scientists and politicians argue that we will not run out of oil in the immediate future. They say there are oil reserves that haven't been discovered yet. They think we have made advances in drilling techniques that make it possible to extract oil that we couldn't reach before. Some experts believe there is enough shale oil to last us thousands of years, but at the moment the cost of extraction is still too high. Oil sands are another potential source that isn't economically viable yet. Other experts believe that extracting shale oil and oil sands is too damaging to the environment.

There is an international consensus and overwhelming scientific evidence that our consumption of fossil fuels is causing global warming. Many scientists and experts predict that extreme weather conditions caused by global warming will plunge the world into an environmental crisis. If we continue to burn fossil fuels at the same rate, they believe the environmental crisis might happen before we run out of fossil fuels. They think we should reduce the consumption of fossil fuels for the sake of the planet and human society.

Oil is not lost! Large reserves of oil sands are currently known to exist in Canada (seen here), Kazakhstan, and Russia.

Action plan

How would you cope if there were an oil crisis? What could you do now to prepare for such an event? Here are a few ideas:

- Travel by bus, train, or bike, or walk more. You're getting to the age when you may be thinking about getting a car. Remember to go for smaller, more fuel-efficient cars.

- Reduce your carbon footprint by not buying as many new products that you don't need, such as gadgets and clothes. They all require energy to manufacture and distribute.

- Reduce your energy consumption. Think about switching off lights and not leaving your computer and other gadgets on stand-by.

- Find out more about alternative energies, such as wind power and solar power. The more you know, the more you can tell other people and try to influence their decisions.

- Grow your own food – you can do this at home or school.

- Consume less and remember the three "Rs": Reduce, Reuse, Recycle!

- Get handy! The more you can do yourself, the less you will need to use electricity! Learn new skills such as sewing by hand or carpentry.

- Get involved! Find out about Transition Movements in your area (see page 46). Join groups and sign petitions that help to bring about change.

"History demonstrates that the deepest and most meaningful cultural/social/political changes began with individuals, not organizations, governments, or institutions."

The Last Hours of Ancient Sunlight by Thom Hartmann (Mobius, 2001)

"We must face the prospect of changing our basic ways of living. This change will either be made on our own initiative in a planned way, or forced on us with chaos and suffering by the inexorable laws of nature."

Jimmy Carter, speaking in 1976, shortly before he became US President. From The Party's Over: Oil, War and the Fate of Industrial Societies by Richard Heinberg (Claireview Books, 2005)

Making the transition

The Transition Movement is based on the idea that local communities need to make a gradual, carefully planned transition towards a fossil-free future. This means looking at every sector of a community, including food, trade, the local economy, housing, heating, education, health, and waste management. It means making plans for a more sustainable future. Some communities have decided to take responsibility and have joined the Transition Movement. The town of Bridport in Dorset became a Transition Town in 2009. Its action plan includes raising awareness, forming work groups and sharing skills, creating sustainable projects in the town, building relationships with the local government, and creating an "energy descent action plan" to reduce energy use.

↘

Get a skill or a trade! You can learn some tricks of the trade like these volunteers on a construction site in New York, USA.

THE FIRST TRANSITION TOWN

Totnes in Devon is no ordinary town. In 2005, it became the first Transitional Town in the world. The people of Totnes aim to become less dependent on fossil fuels and reduce carbon emissions, while strengthening the local economy and becoming more self-reliant in producing food, energy, and services. Initiatives include turning the town car park into a market garden and installing solar panels on civic buildings. Totnes has become the model for transitional initiatives all around the world. It may well set the template for how we should live in the future.

The future

Nobody knows for certain what will happen in the world after fossil fuels run out. We can't even be sure when or if it will happen. In this book, we have explored what could happen in an oil crisis and the knock-on effect this could have on the use of fossil fuels. It is unlikely that we will completely run out of fossil fuels in the near future, but the clock is ticking and governments around the world are seeking alternative energy solutions.

Technology holds the key. Some scientists believe nuclear fusion is the key to a limitless supply of clean energy. Others think the answer lies out in space: one day it may be possible to source nuclear fuel from the Moon or have space-based solar power stations. Even further into the future, when fossil fuels are depleted, will there be human colonization of space? Plans for space tourism exist now – will this lead to permanent space colonies? Some of these ideas may sound like science fiction, but sci-fi predictions often have a way of coming true.

↖

Space may hold the key to our future energy needs. The skies above could one day be filled with solar-powered satellites using energy from the Sun.

WRITE YOUR OWN STORY

You may have already thought about a world after fossil fuels or it may be an entirely new idea to you. A world like this has been described by many writers, and you could write your own view of how people would live in a world without fossil fuels.

Inspiration

First, you will need inspiration. This simple exercise will soon get the creative juices flowing: think about the countless ways that petrol or oil affects your life.

You may start off with basics such as the clothes on your back and the food you eat. How would an oil crisis affect the supply of food and clothes? Very soon, you may be asking questions such as: "What would I do if there were no more essentials left at my local shop?" Imagine what you would do in this scenario. What would other people do? Describe some possible outcomes. Expand your scenario to include other aspects of daily life, such as school, work, health, and entertainment.

Research

Over the next few weeks, make sure you take a notepad out with you. Hopefully, new ideas will come to you when you're going about your daily life. Talk to friends and family about the subject and note down any interesting ideas. Watch the world around you and write down your observations. Read around the subject and begin to research your ideas. Try to understand how far technology relies on fossil fuels, and the potential difficulties and pitfalls of relying on certain types of technology.

Delve into fiction, non-fiction, magazine and newspaper articles, and browse the internet. Watch films or dramas about world crises. Absorb all kinds of information and it will help to shape your story.

The plot

Once you have an idea for your story, you may be tempted to start writing straight away. However, it's a good idea to write a plot and plan the basics of the story. A good plot needs an introduction, action, a climatic event, and a conclusion. You may have a great idea for an ending but don't know how to start the story. Don't let this stop you from getting on with writing the plot. Let your imagination go to work, but always have the plot in mind.

Background information

A good story needs strong settings. A story after fossil fuels runs out will probably be set in the future. Think about how far into the future this is going to be. A book set in the immediate future needs to feel realistic in the situations, technology, and behaviour of the people it describes. The notes you kept will come in handy for this. If the book is set in hundreds of years' time, your imagination can go wild. However, write down as much of the background information as possible so that when you begin writing your story it will be consistent.

Characters

Interesting characters are key to a good read. The conflict between the "heroes" and the "bad guys" often drives a good story, but try to make it believable. Make a character list before you begin, noting personality traits, appearances, backgrounds, and relationships. You may not include all this in the story but it will help you to get to know the characters before you start writing.

Once you have as much background as possible then start writing. That first page is crucial. Work on it until you're sure you have a gripping introduction. From there, let the plot guide the way and allow your imagination to do the rest. Writing isn't easy, so don't give up. Good luck!

TIMELINE

16 March 2020

Car bombs are detonated in Riyadh, Saudi Arabia, killing 30 people

19 March 2020

Suicide bombers kill hundreds of Westerners and Saudis living in Riyadh, Saudi Arabia

20 March 2020

Terrorists begin attacking oil tankers in the Strait of Hormuz in the Persian Gulf

21 March 2020 – September 2020

Terrorists make surprise attacks against oil tankers in the Persian Gulf, bringing the export of oil from the Gulf to non-Arabic nations to a virtual standstill

21 March 2020

Large queues at petrol stations are reported all around the world. Certain news reports suggest there is a "Global Oil Crisis", while other news sources urge people not to panic buy fuel.

21 March 2020

Emergency talks are held in government offices around the world to work out the severity of the situation

24 March 2020

There are reports of some fuel stations running out of petrol a few days into the crisis because of panic buying. World leaders begin crisis talks amid mounting fears of actual oil shortages. People begin panic buying staples such as bread. Airlines cancelling flights and non-emergency flights are delayed.

4 April 2020

Petrol becomes a scarce resource and more than quadruples in price in most places. Fuel fury and fuel theft are on the increase. Protests are held outside government buildings and oil refineries around the world.

5 April 2020

Traffic organizations report a decrease in the number of vehicles on the roads. Lorries are unable to deliver goods. In a poll in the United States, over half of corporations suggest that less than 50 per cent of its workforce are able to make the commute to their work.

6 April 2020

Serious food shortages at supermarkets and food outlets mean that some governments are forced to introduce emergency measures such as the rationing of staple food

10 April 2020

Less than a month after the crisis started, some governments have introduced curfews to maintain public order

11 April 2020

Airlines are at a virtual standstill apart from emergency traffic. Goods and passenger trains are cancelled or running a skeleton service. Undelivered cargo is piling up at airports and railway goods stations.

20 April 2020

Small and large businesses are struggling to cope in the crisis and many have gone under, causing more shortages

21 April 2020

Power cuts and blackouts are reported in most countries as some national grids struggle to cope

June 2020

Government leaders work around the clock to find a way to handle the energy crisis in the long term. Many leaders understand that they need to invest in more non-renewable energy sources.

2021

The world is in economic meltdown and many nations face economic collapse. Industry and manufacturing is in crisis.

Oil-rich nations in the Middle East, Russia, and China are coping much better.

Food production is in crisis and nations that previously relied upon imported staple foodstuffs have greater shortages. More nations are introducing food rationing to help manage the situation.

The supply of safe, clean drinking water is an issue around the world. Desert cities like Las Vegas and Los Angeles have become virtual ghost towns because of water shortages.

Health services around the globe are seriously disrupted. Many hospitals are prioritizing emergency treatment.

Fossil-free cities that have developed sustainable ways of living, such as Växjö in Sweden, have become the blueprint for developments around the world.

2025

World demography changes as millions of people migrate to different countries or areas that have managed the transition to renewable resources and adapted their lifestyles.

Everyday life changes for everyone: consumerism is a thing of the past. Many families do not have a vehicle; they use bicycles or rely upon public transport networks. There is more acceptance of the situation and people don't expect life to return to normal – they are making new lives for themselves.

Many small communities around the world are successfully feeding themselves and sustaining their communities.

For industry and manufacturing the focus is now on energy efficient technology.

Social commentators call this the "New Age" – it is a time of innovation and community spirit.

GLOSSARY

anaerobic digester method of breaking down and treating biodegradable waste without the need for oxygen. Micro-organisms break down the waste into a nutrient-rich organic matter that can be used to improve soil.

biodegradable able to rot away over time

biofuel fuel made from plants

biomass plant material or animal waste that is burned to create energy

black market illegal trading of rationed goods or goods in scarce supply

blockade prevents something, such as fuel, entering or exiting an area, for example, a harbour or oil refinery

carbon dioxide gas that is given off when fossil fuels, such as coal, oil, and natural gas, are burned. It is called a greenhouse gas because it traps heat from the Sun in Earth's atmosphere and adds to the greenhouse effect.

Chernobyl disaster accident at the Chernobyl nuclear power station in the Soviet Union on 25 April 1986. The fire and explosion at the plant caused radioactive material to be released into the atmosphere. The impact of the accident is still debated but an area roughly 31 kilometres (19 miles) around the plant remains an exclusion zone over 25 years after the disaster.

composter container in which waste vegetable matter is collected and converted to compost

consumerism over-attachment to material possessions which leads to greater spending and consumption of goods

crude oil oil as it is found naturally under ground

curfew regulation requiring people to remain indoors between certain hours

diesel fuel obtained from crude oil that is similar to petrol

generator machine that turns the energy of movement into electricity

geologist professional person who studies the geological features of Earth

geothermal heat heat from deep under the ground, such as hot springs

global warming rise in the average temperature of Earth's atmosphere

hydropower electricity that is generated from the energy of running water, usually by a power station built on a dam across a river

Industrial Revolution rapid development of industry in Europe during the late 18th and 19th centuries, brought about by the introduction of machinery, steam power, and the growth of factories

insulation protective layers of material used to trap heat and prevent it from escaping

national grid network of electric power lines in a particular country

non-renewable resources resources that cannot be replaced

offshore in the sea not far from the coast

oil refinery industrial plant where oil is processed and purified

OPEC (Organization of the Petroleum Exporting Countries) organization created in 1960 including the nations of Iran, Iraq, Kuwait, and Saudi Arabia. Since then other members have included Qatar, Libya, Algeria, and Nigeria. The organization's objectives include co-ordinating and unifying policies on petroleum to secure fair and stable prices for its members.

photovoltaic relating to the generation of electricity from the Sun

radioactive emits harmful radiation rays

renewable resources source of energy, such as water, wind, or solar power, that can never be used up

scarcity when goods are in short supply and cannot meet demand

sustainable something that can be maintained without depleting natural resources

template something that is a model or guide for others to copy

FIND OUT MORE

Non-fiction books

Biomass Power (Energy Debate), Isabel Thomas (Wayland, 2009)

Energy (DK Eyewitness Books), Jack Challoner (DK, 2012)

Fossil Fuels (Energy Now and in the Future), Neil Morris (Franklin Watts, 2006)

Future Energy (British Issues), Andrea Smith (Franklin Watts, 2007)

Fiction books

Ship Breaker, Paolo Bacigalupi (Atom, 2011)

The Changes: The Weathermonger, Peter Dickinson (Collins, 1968)

The Road, Cormac McCarthy (Picador, 2009)

The Water Wars, Cameron Stracher (Sourcebooks Fire, 2011)

Websites

www.britishwindenergy.co.uk
The British Wind Energy Association's website has lots of information about the benefits of wind power.

www.carbonkids.net/kids_fossilfuels.html
This site is packed full of information, games, and activities that help students to understand how our daily lives and consumption of fossil fuels affect the environment.

www.ewea.org
Learn more about wind energy on the European Wind Energy Association's website.

kids.everykilowattcounts.ca/en/whats-my-electric-personality/personality_quiz.aspx
Discover your "electric" personality with this fun questionnaire and discover some energy saving ways.

www.greenpeace.org.uk/oil
Greenpeace advises people to go beyond oil for the health of the planet.

www.transitionnetwork.org
Find out about the network for communities adapting to a transition model.

Topics to research

Design a Car of the Future

Research and design your own vehicle of the future. Explore different ideas such as solar-powered cars or vehicles that utilize magnets for motion. Investigate the kinds of vehicles that are already being designed and presented at car shows now. Play with ideas and think about different ways of generating the energy to power cars. Think about energy efficiency and how this car would operate in a world after fossil fuels run out.

Next, think about the design of the car and the features it will need to make it even more efficient. The final step is to design the vehicle. You could do this on paper or on a computer. This is an activity you may enjoy at home but it could work well in class as a group activity, too. At school there would be more opportunities for group discussion and evaluation of the different designs. Making a model of the car would be a great extension of this activity.

Businesses of the Future

Imagine yourself living in a world after fossil fuels. What kinds of jobs and careers will people have? How will workers make a living? What types of businesses will there be? The world will be a much more uncertain place. Think about the jobs and skills that you would need in this situation.

If you were to set up your own enterprise or business what would it be? Why do you think it would work and how would you start up this business? Is your idea realistic and could it make money? What would the risks be and how would you make your business succeed? This would make a good group activity that allows you to explore ideas together. Once you have discussed and investigated your ideas, write a business plan.

INDEX